Fast Reference Guide
to Programming
dBASE II®

John D. McCharen
MicroComputer Education, Inc.

HAYDEN BOOK COMPANY, INC.
Hasbrouck Heights, New Jersey

Acquisitions Editor: DOUGLAS McCORMICK
Production Editor: MAUREEN CONNELLY
Art Director: JIM BERNARD
Composition: ART, COPY, AND PRINT, INC.
Printed and bound by: COMMAND WEB OFFSET, INC.

dBASE II is a registered trademark of Ashton Tate, Inc.

	2	3	4	5	6	7	8	9	PRINTING
84	85	86	87	88	89	90	91	92	YEAR

This reference guide is one of a two-volume set for dBASE II. A fast reference to all dBASE II functions and commands is included in this volume. A detailed reference is provided for all functions but only for those commands which are commonly invoked from command files rather than a terminal. A detailed reference for the other dBASE II commands is found in the *Fast Reference Guide to Using dBASE II*.

Files

dBASE filenames are 1 to 8 characters optionally prefixed by a
disk drive and optionally suffixed by a filetype.

The optional drive letter followed by a colon (:) is the letter of
the system drive where the file resides. If it is not specified, the
dBASE **DEFAULT** drive is assumed. If the filetype is not specified
by the user, dBASE assumes it to be one of the following:

.DBF — database file
.MEM — memory file
.CMD — command file
.FRM — report form file
.TXT — text output file
.NDX — index file
.FMT — format file

Command Format Notation

[ ] Brackets: Items within square brackets are optional.
< > Braces: Items within pointed braces are variables supplied
by the user.
boldface: Items in boldface are keywords which are written as
shown.

Variables and Constants (or Literals)

dBASE supports three types of variables and constants:

- character
- numeric
- logical or boolean

Variables are specified by database field names or memory
variable names.

Character constants are specified as a character string
enclosed in single quotes (') or double quotes (").

Numeric constants are specified with an optional sign, decimal digits, and an optional decimal point.

Boolean constants are represented by T, t, Y, y for true, and by F, f, N, n for false.

Arithmetic Operators

+   addition
−   subtraction
*   multiplication
/   division

Boolean Operators

.OR.   boolean or
.AND.   boolean and
.NOT.   boolean negation

Character String Operators

+   string concatenation
−   string concatenation with the removal of blanks

Relational Operators

<   less than
>   greater than
=   equal to
not equal to
<=   less than or equal to
>=   greater than or equal to
$ a substring of

Expressions

dBASE II supports logical, numeric, and character expressions. Expressions are formed with literals, variables, functions, and the appropriate operators.

Macro Substitution

An ampersand (&) followed by a character string memory variable is replaced by the contents of the variable. The memory variable may be terminated by a period (.) to remove any ambiguity.

Command Files

Command files are files of type .CMD consisting of a sequence of dBASE II commands. They are invoked from the terminal or from within a command file by the **DO** command.

Continuation of Commands

A command may be continued to another line from within a command file by means of a semicolon (;).

Full Screen Operations—Normal

CTRL-E,A	moves cursor to the previous field
CTRL-X,F	moves cursor to the next field
CTRL-S	moves cursor to previous character
CTRL-D	moves cursor to next character

CTRL-Y	clears the current field
CTRL-V	toggles between replace and insert mode
CTRL-G	deletes the character at the cursor
DEL	deletes the character prior to the cursor
CTRL-Q	quits full screen editing

Full Screen Operations—with Browse

CTRL-Z	shifts the screen left one field
CTRL-B	shifts the screen right one field
CTRL-R	moves the cursor up one record
CTRL-C	moves the cursor down one record
CTRL-U	marks/unmarks the current record for deletion
CTRL-Q	exits without saving any changes
CTRL-W	exits and writes the changes to disk

Full Screen Operations—with Modify

CTRL-N	inserts a blank line at the cursor position
CTRL-T	deletes a line at the cursor position
CTRL-C	scrolls up
CTRL-R	scrolls down
CTRL-W	exits and writes the changes to disk
CTRL-Q	exits without saving any changes

Full Screen Operations—with Edit

CTRL-U	marks/unmarks the record for deletion
CTRL-R	writes current record and positions to previous record
CTRL-C	writes current record and positions to next record
CTRL-W	writes current record and exits

Full Screen Operations
—with Append, Create, Insert

CTRL-C,R	writes the current record to disk and proceeds to the next
<Carriage Return>	terminate operation when cursor is in initial position and no changes have been made

The Functions—Fast Reference

#

returns the current position.

$(<character expression>,<start>,<length>)

returns a substring of the given character expression.

*

returns logical true if the current record has been marked for deletion.

@(<character expression 1>,<character expression 2>)

returns an integer representing the location of the first occurrence of the first string in the second, or 0.

!(<character expression>)

converts the character string expression to uppercase.

CHR(<numeric expression>)

converts the numeric expression to the ASCII character equivalent.

DATE()

returns the system date in the form mm/dd/yy.

EOF

returns logical true if end of file exists.

FILE(<character expression>)

returns logical true if the character string exists in the directory.

INT(<numeric expression>)

returns the greatest integer value.

LEN(<character expression>)

returns the length of a character string.

STR(<numeric expression>,<length>[,<precision>])

returns a character string representing the numeric expression.

TRIM(<character expression>)

removes trailing blanks from the character string expression.

VAL(<character expression>)

returns an integer from the character string made up of a sign digit and up to one decimal point.

TYPE(<expression>)

returns the type of expression: numeric, character, or boolean.

The Commands—Fast Reference

?

Displays the value(s) of a list of expressions.

Displays formatted information on the screen or printer. In

conjunction with its options and other commands, it is useful for conversing with the terminal.

ACCEPT

Accepts a character string from the terminal and assigns it to a memory variable.

APPEND

Appends records to the database in use. The data may be entered from the terminal or extracted from another file or database.

BROWSE

Allows "browsing" through the database. Data from up to nineteen records at a time is displayed on the screen with forward and backward scrolling permitted. Selected data may be edited.

CANCEL

Cancel the execution of a command file.

CHANGE

Allows the change of selected fields from selected records of the database in use.

CLEAR

Either clears outstanding **GET**s used in conjunction with the **@** command, or resets dBASE II. In the latter case, all databases in use are closed, all memory variables are released, and the primary work area is selected.

CONTINUE

Continues the search initiated by the **LOCATE** command.

COPY

Copies a database to another database or unloads the database to a file in the system data format. In the latter case, the fields of the records may or may not be delimited as desired.

COUNT

Counts selected records of the database in use.

CREATE

Creates a database structure. Data may or may not be entered at the time of creation.

DELETE

Marks selected records for deletion. The records may then be physically deleted with a **PACK** command or may be recovered with a **RECALL** command. Alternatively, an entire file may be deleted.

DISPLAY

Displays selected records from the database in use, or the structure of the database in use, or the contents of all memory variables, or the names of files on the default disk.

DO

Used to execute a command file and to implement the "do while" or "case" constructs within a command file.

EDIT

Allows for the editing of selected fields of the data base.

EJECT

Issues a form feed to the printer when used in conjunction with various print operations.

ENDCASE

Marks the end of the "case" construct.

ENDDO

Marks the end of a "do while" construct.

ENDIF

Marks the end of an "if ... else" construct.

ERASE

Clears the screen and positions the cursor to upper corner of the screen. Also clears memory of any prior @ command gets and pictures.

FIND

Finds the first occurrence of a record having a given key in an indexed data base.

GO
GOTO

Changes the current position in the database to a specified location.

IF

Used to implement the "if ... else" construct.

INDEX

Creates an index on a specified key for the database in use.

INPUT

Prompts for input from the terminal to a specified memory variable.

INSERT

Inserts a record into the database in use.

JOIN

Creates a "join" of the primary and secondary databases. (See the detailed reference for a description of *join*).

LIST

Lists the records of the database in use, or the structure of the data base in use, or the contents of all memory variables, or files in the directory.

LOCATE

Locates a specified record in the data base. May be used in conjunction with the **CONTINUE** command.

LOOP

Used from within a **DO WHILE** loop to cause control to be passed to the **DO WHILE**.

MODIFY

Allows for the modification of a database structure or a command file.

NOTE
*

Denotes a comment within a command file. An asterisk (*) may also be used.

PACK

Removes records marked for deletion by the **DELETE** command. These records are not recoverable.

QUIT

Closes all files and returns control to the operating system.

READ

Reads data from the terminal as specified by the **GET** phrase within previously issued @ commands. Full-screen editing is allowed.

RECALL

Recovers records which have been marked for deletion by the **DELETE** command.

RELEASE

Releases selected memory variables.

REMARK

Echoes comments to the screen during the execution of a command file.

RENAME

Renames a file within the directory.

REPLACE

Replaces data within specified portions of the database.

REPORT

Creates a report form or invokes a previously created form. This is a quick way of producing simple reports without creating a command file.

RETURN

Exits a command file returning control to the invoking command file or to the terminal, if the command file was invoked directly from the terminal.

RESTORE

Reads a memory file previously saved with a **SAVE** command. The variables within this file become the current memory variables.

SAVE

Writes the current memory variables to a memory file. This file may be subsequently read by issuing a **RESTORE** command.

SELECT

Allows the user to select a primary or a secondary database for use in subsequent commands.

SET

Sets the selected dBASE II switch **ON** or **OFF**. It is also used to set other global variables.

SKIP

Skips forward or backward through the database; i.e., changes current position.

SORT

Produces a sorted copy of a database on a given field.

STORE

Stores a value in a specified memory variable.

SUM

Sums selected fields from the database in use.

TOTAL

Computes subtotals and places them in a database.

UPDATE

Updates selected records from the database in use with data of another database.

USE

Specifies the database to be used and any associated index files.

WAIT

Waits until a single character is entered from the keyboard.

The Functions—Detailed Reference

#

Returns the value of current position of the database in use. This is an integer record number.

$(<character expression>,<start>,<length>)

Returns a substring of the character expression.

where: **<character expression>** is a character expression.

<start> specifies the beginning location of the substring within the character expression. It may be specified by a numeric literal, variable, or expression.

<length> specifies the length of the substring. It may be specified by a numeric literal, variable, or expression.

notes: When this function is used to generate a key for an index, **<start>** and **<length** must be specified by literals.

If there are not enough characters in the **<character expression>** to fill out the substring as specified by **<length>**, then a short substring is returned.

examples: **$('hotdog',4,3)**   returns **dog**

$('copycat',5,4)   returns **cat** (a short substring)

ACCEPT "enter the date MM/DD/YY" TO DATE
STORE $(DATE,1,2) TO MONTH
STORE $(DATE,4,2) TO DAY
STORE $(DATE,7,2) TO YEAR

Here the substring function is used to isolate the month, day, and year of a character string entered from the terminal. Similar examples could be given to isolate the primary and secondary characters of a part number, account number, or other similar types of data entered from the terminal.

LIST FOR $(PHONE:NUM,1,3)='815'

Lists those records of the database for which the area code portion of the phone number field, **PHONE:NUM**, is **815**.

Returns logical true if the current record of the database in use has been marked for deletion.

LOCATE FOR *
IF STATUS'PAID'
   RECALL
ENDIF

Locates a record marked for deletion and unmarks it, if the **STATUS** field indicates **PAID**.

@(<character expression 1>,<character expression 2>)

Returns an integer representing the location of the first character expression in the second. Zero is returned if the first expression is not a substring of the second.

where: **<character expression 1-2>** are character expressions.

examples: **@('hot','hotdog')**   returns 1
              @('dog','hotdog')   returns 4
              @('cat','hotdog')   returns 0

!(<character expression>)

Returns a string containing the characters of the character expression in uppercase.

where: **<character expression>** is a character expression.
notes: This is useful for allowing the user to enter data from the terminal without regard for case.
examples: **!(hot)**   returns **HOT**

ACCEPT "do you wish to continue
   (Y/N)" TO FLAG
IF !(FLAG) = 'N'
   CANCEL
ENDIF

Here the user is allowed to enter an uppercase **N** or a lowercase **n**. The input value is tested for an uppercase **N** after translating the input character to uppercase.

CHR(<numeric expression>)

Returns the ASCII equivalent of the numeric expression.

where: **<numeric expression>** is a numeric expression.

notes: This is used for sending ASCII characters to devices such as the printer.

examples: **CHR(13)** returns an ASCII line feed

NAME+CHR(13)+STREET+CHR(13)+CITY+ STATE+ZIP

Causes three lines to be printed if directed to the printer.

DATE()

Returns a character string containing the date in the format MM/DD/YY.

REPLACE OPEN:DATE WITH DATE()

Replace the **OPEN:DATE** field of the current record with the current system date.

EOF

Returns logical true if the end of file condition exists.

examples: **LOCATE FOR STATUS='UNPAID'**
IF .NOT. EOF
    DELETE
ENDIF

Locates a record whose status field is UNPAID and marks it for deletion if EOF was not encountered.

FILE(<character expression>)

Returns logical true if the character expression matches an entry in the directory of the dBASE II default disk.

notes: If the drive is not specified, the **DEFAULT** drive is assumed.

examples: **FILE('B:DBASE.TXT')**   example
FILE('A:DBASE.COM')   syntax
FILE('PIP.COM')   usage

ACCEPT 'enter file name' TO DB
IF FILE(!(DB))
    USE &DB
ENDIF

Accepts the name of a database from the terminal and puts it in the memory variable **DB**. If the data base is in the directory it is **USE**d.

INT(<numeric expression>)

Returns the greatest integer less than or equal to the value of the numeric expression.

where: **<numeric expression>** is a numeric expression.

example: **INT(4.34)**   evaluates to 4
             INT(7)   evaluates to 7

LEN(<character expression>)

Returns the length of the character expression.

where: **<character> expression** is a character expression.

examples: **LEN('CUST.DBF')**   returns **8**

STR(<numeric expression>,<length>[,<precision>])

Returns a character string of decimal digits representing a numeric expression. The arguments are literals, variables, or numeric expressions.

where: **<numeric expression>** is a numeric expression.

             <length> is the length of the character string, including the decimal point.

             <precision> is the number of digits to the right of the decimal point. The default is 0.

notes: Leading zeros are replaced with blanks.

             Digits are truncated or padded with zeros to the right of the decimal point as necessary.

             Asterisks (*) are returned if significant digits are lost to the left of the decimal point.

             The function is useful for the "concatenation" of character and numeric fields for indexing purposes.

examples: Suppose **NUMBER** is a field of the database in use having a value **0234.5678**. Then

STR(number,9,4) has a value **234.5678**
(one leading blank)
STR(number,8,2) has a value **234.56**
(two leading blanks)
STR(number,9,5) has a value **234.56780**
(no leading blanks)

INDEX ON STR(AMOUNT,9,2)+LAST:NAME

Indexes the database in use on the concatenation of the character representation of the **AMOUNT** field with the **LAST:NAME** field.

TRIM(<character expression>)

Returns a character string with trailing blanks removed.

where: **<character expression>** is a character expression.

notes: **TRIM** cannot be used as part of the key definition of the **INDEX** command.

examples: **TRIM('hello   ')+':'** has a value **hello:**

**@ 10,1 SAY TRIM(FIRST:NAME)+' '+
TRIM(LAST:NAME)**

Outputs a formatted name to the display.

TYPE(<expression>)

Returns a one character string representing the type of the expression—**L** for logical, **N** for numeric, or **C** for character.

where: **<expression>** is a logical, numeric, or character expression.

examples: **TYPE(123)**   returns **N**
TYPE('CUST.TXT')   returns **C**
TYPE('SMITH'$!(NAME))   returns **L**

VAL(<character expression>)

Converts a character string containing an optional sign, decimal digits, and an optional decimal point into an integer. That is, **VAL** returns an integer numeric value represented by the character string.

notes: The scan of the **<character expression>** is terminated by the first nondecimal digit following the optional sign.

This allows arithmetic to be done with character fields that happen to contain numeric digits, e.g., a time or date field.

example: **VAL('123.24')**   returns **123**

VAL('123xxx')   returns **123**

Suppose that **TIME** represents the time in the form **HH:MM:SS**.

$(1,2)   returns **HH**, so

VAL($(1,2))+1   represents the hours plus 1

The Commands—Detailed Reference

? [<expression list>]
?? [<expression list>]

Evaluates and displays a list of expressions. A single **?** performs a line feed before displaying the list. The **??** does not.

where: **<expression list>** is a list of expressions separated by commas. They may be logical, numeric, or character expression.

examples: • **? NAME**   Will output the **NAME** field of the current record.
• **? #**   Will output the current record number.
• **? 5+10**   Will output **15**.
• **? 1=2**   Will output **.F.** for logical false

notes: A **?** with no operands simply performs the line feed. This is useful in command files for creating blank lines on the output device.

@ <row,column>   [SAY <expression>] [USING <picture>]
[GET <variable>] [PICTURE <picture>]

Displays formatted output on the output device. When used with the **GET** phrase and **READ** command, it provides formatted output and input from the terminal.

where:　　　**<row,column>** specifies coordinates for cursor positioning. Each coordinate may be expressed as a literal, a numeric memory variable, or a numeric expression. For screen output, the range is 0–24 for the row and 0–79 for the column. For printer output, the range is 0–254 for both the row and column.

SAY <expression> denotes an expression to be displayed at the cursor position. In the absence of the **USING** phrase, dBASE II formats the output according to its type.

USING <picture> defines the format of the output data.

GET <variable> displays the indicated variable on the output device. **<variable>** is either a character memory variable or a database field name. If output is directed to the screen, it may be edited by issuing a **READ** command. In the absence of the **PICTURE** phrase, dBASE II will format the output and subsequent input according to its type.

PICTURE <picture> defines the format of the output data and any subsequent input.

<picture> is a character string enclosed in quotes ('). **9**s or **#**s represent numeric data, **X**s alphanumeric data, and **A**s alphabetic data. In addition, ***** or **$** may be used in specifying numeric fields to cause leading zeros to be replaced by an ***** or **$**. An **!** may be used instead of **X** or **A** to convert lowercase to uppercase.

The following commands are used in conjunction with the @ command:

SET INTENSITY ON affects the screen intensity of **GET**s and **SAY**s.

SET BELL ON causes the bell to ring when invalid data is entered or data boundaries are crossed when the **GET**s are being edited by a **READ** command.

SET DEBUG ON causes output from the **ECHO** and **STEP** features to be routed to the printer.

SET PRINT ON sends output to the printer.

SET SCREEN ON allows full-screen editing.

SET FORMAT TO SCREEN causes output from **@** commands to be routed to the screen.

SET FORMAT TO PRINT causes output from **@** commands to be routed to the printer.

SET FORMAT TO <format file> specifies a file as the source of **@** commands for the **READ** command.

READ causes editing mode to be entered for all outstanding **GET**s. If a **SET FORMAT TO** <format file> has been issued, then all **@** commands in the format file are executed prior to the execution of **READ**.

notes: Any character other than **#**, **9**, **X**, **A**, **$**, *****, or **!** is considered a special character when used in the **USING** <picture> phrase and is sent to the output device as encountered without losing any characters or digits of the **SAY** <expression>.

Any character other than **#**, **9**, **X**, **A**, **$**, *****, or **!** is considered a special character when used in the **PICTURE** <picture> phrase and is sent to the output device when encountered. When the **GET** <variable> is edited via a **READ** command, such characters are protected.

Up to 64 **GET**s may be outstanding before issuing a **READ** command to clear them.

If **SET PRINT ON** has been issued causing output to be sent to the printer, then it is not necessary to issue a **READ** command to clear the **GET**s.

examples: **. SET COLON ON**
. STORE '8158956401' TO PHONE
. @ 10,10 SAY PHONE USING '(XXX)
XXX-XXXX'

causes :**(815) 895-6401**: to be displayed.

. STORE '
TO PHONE
. @ 10,10 GET PHONE PICTURE '(XXX)
XXX-XXXX'

causes :(   )   –   : to be displayed. When the **READ** command is issued, the cursor is positioned to the second character of the field since the **(** is protected.

Suppose **NUMBER** is a numeric field of length 9, including the decimal point, containing 4 decimal places, and having a value 0123.4567.

. @ 10,10 say number using '9999.9999'

causes **123.4567** to be displayed, suppressing the leading zero. Note the use of the decimal point.

ACCEPT [<prompt string>] TO <memory variable>

Creates a character memory variable and assigns input from the terminal to it.

where: **<prompt string>** is a string of characters enclosed in quotes ('), double quotes ("), or brackets ([]) for prompting the user. If they are omitted, the user is prompted with a colon (:).

<memory variable< is the name of the memory variable in which to place the input character string.

notes: If only a carriage return is entered in response to the prompt, a single blank is assigned to the memory variable.

The user does not enclose the data in quotes as with the **INPUT** command,

example: **ACCEPT "enter database" TO DB**
USE &DB

Accepts a database name from the terminal and uses the database.

APPEND BLANK

Appends a space filled record to the data base in use.
examples: **ERASE**
APPEND BLANK
@ 1,1 SAY "enter name   " GET NAME
@ 3,1 SAY "enter amount " GET AMOUNT
READ
REPLACE DEPOSITS WITH AMOUNT,
BALANCE WITH AMOUNT,WITHDRAWAL;
WITH 0
@ 23,1 SAY "add complete"

Appends a space filled record to the database in use. The **NAME** and **AMOUNT** fields are filled in via the **READ** command. Then the **DEPOSITS** and **BALANCE** fields are filled with the **AMOUNT**, and the **WITHDRAWAL** field is filled with **0**. The point is that a record was added to the database, filling in some fields from the terminal and assigning default values to others. Note the use of the semicolon to continue the **REPLACE** command to a second line.

CANCEL

Cancels the execution of a command file and any invoking command file and returns to normal dBASE II interpretive mode.

CLEAR
CLEAR GETS

CLEAR resets dBASE II. All databases are closed, memory variables are released, and the primary work area is selected.

CLEAR GETS clears any pending **GET**s, leaving the screen intact.

notes: A **CLEAR** may be issued at the beginning of a command file to give dBASE II a known state.

DO <command file>

DO WHILE <expression>
    <commands>
ENDDO

DO CASE
    CASE <expression>
        <commands>
    CASE <expression>
        <commands>
    .
    .
    .
    [OTHERWISE]
        <commands>
ENDCASE

The **DO** causes the specified command file to be executed. It may be used in command files, thus allowing them to be nested.

DO WHILE is used to implement the "do while" construct within command files. While **<expression>** is true, all **<commands>** between the **DO WHILE** and the matching **ENDDO** are executed.

DO CASE is used to implement the "case" structure. All **CASE** phrases are scanned until one having a true **<expression>** is found. Then all **<commands>** between this **CASE** and the next delimiting phrase (**CASE**, **OTHERWISE,** or **ENDCASE**) are executed. If none of the expressions are true, and the **OTHERWISE** phrase is present, then those **<commands>** between the **OTHER-WISE** and the **ENDCASE** are executed. If none of the expressions are true and the **OTHERWISE** is not present, then nothing is executed.

where: **<expression>** is a logical expression.

<commands> represents a sequence of commands.

notes: Only those **<commands>** associated with the first **CASE** for which **<expression>** is true are executed.

examples: **DO MENU**

Causes a command file called **MENU** to be executed. This command file might have the following structure:

```
CLEAR
@ 2,10 SAY "DATA BASE UPDATE MENU"
@ 4,1 SAY "SUPPORTED TRANSACTIONS FOLLOW"
@ 6,4 SAY "1 - ADD A RECORD"
@ 7,4 SAY "2 - CHANGE A RECORD"
@ 8,4 SAY "3 - DELETE A RECORD"
@ 9,4 SAY "4 - EXIT TO dBASE II"
@ 13,1 SAY "ENTER THE TRANSACTION NUMBER"
WAIT TO XACT
DO WHILE XACT # "4"
    DO CASE
        CASE XACT = "1"
            DO ADD
        CASE XACT = "2"
            DO CHANGE
        CASE XACT = "3"
            DO ALTER
        OTHERWISE
            @ 23,1 SAY "INVALID TRANSACTION"
    ENDCASE
    @ 13,1 SAY "ENTER THE TRANSACTION NUMBER"
    WAIT TO XACT
    @ 23,1
ENDDO
@ 23,1 SAY "GOOD BYE"
RETURN
```

EJECT

If **SET PRINT ON** or **SET FORMAT TO PRINT** has been issued, this causes a form feed to be sent to the printer. The "row" and "column" registers are also cleared.

notes: Clearing the row and column registers is significant when output is being directed to the printer via @ commands.

ENDDO

Marks the end of the **DO WHILE** construct. (See the **DO** command.)

ENDCASE

Marks the end of the **DO CASE** construct. (See the **DO** command.)

ENDIF

Marks the end of the **IF ... ELSE** construct. (See the **IF** command.)

ERASE

Clears all pending **GET**s associated with prior **@** commands, clears the screen, and positions the cursor at the home position.

notes: **CLEAR GETS** clears pending gets while leaving the screen intact. (See the **CLEAR** command.)

IF <expression>
   <commands>
[ELSE
   <commands>]
ENDIF

Implements the "if ... else" construct. If **<expression>** is true, then those **<commands>** between the **IF** and the **ELSE** are executed. Otherwise, the **<commands>** following the **ELSE** and prior to the **ENDIF** are executed. If **<expression>** is false and the **ELSE** is omitted, the **<commands>** are not executed.

where: **<expression>** denotes a logical expression.
           <commands> denotes a sequence of commands.

INPUT [<prompt string>] TO <memory variable>

Allows expression values to be assigned to the specified memory variable. Logical, numeric, and character expressions may be entered from the terminal.

where: **<prompt string>** is a character string delimited by quotes ('), double quotes ("), or brackets ([]) used to prompt the user for input.
           TO <memory variable> defines the memory variable to receive the input.
note: The type of memory variable created is determined by the user input. A character, numeric, or logical variable is created according to whether a character, numeric, or logical expression is entered.

T or Y may be entered for logical true and F or N for logical false.

Character strings must be delimited by quotes ('), double quotes ("), or brackets ([]).

The **TYPE** function may be used to determine the type of memory variable created.

The **ACCEPT** is a more convenient way to enter a character constant.

examples: **3+4** entered in response to **INPUT TO X** will create a numeric memory variable **X** having value **7**.

"c"+"a"+"t" entered in response to **INPUT TO X** will create a character memory variable **X** having value **cat**.

1=2 entered in response to **INPUT TO X** will create a logical memory variable having value **.F.** or false.

INSERT [BEFORE] [BLANK]

Inserts a record into the database in use.

where: **BEFORE** indicates that the record is to be inserted before the current record. If not written, the record will be inserted after the current record.

BLANK will cause a space filled record to be inserted into the database. If not written, the user is prompted to enter the data.

example: **ERASE**
INSERT BLANK
@ 1,1 SAY "enter name "   GET NAME
@ 3,1 SAY "enter amount " GET AMOUNT
READ
REPLACE DEPOSITS WITH AMOUNT, BALANCE WITH AMOUNT,WITHDRAW-AL; WITH 0
@ 23,1 SAY "insert complete"

Inserts a space filled record to the database in use. The **NAME** and **AMOUNT** fields are filled in via the **READ** command. Then the **DEPOSITS** and **BALANCE** fields are filled with the **AMOUNT**, and the **WITHDRAWAL** field is filled with **0**. The point is that a record was added to the database filling in some fields from the terminal and assigning default values to others. Note the use of the semicolon to continue the **REPLACE** command to a second line.

LOOP

Is used within a **DO WHILE** construct to cause control to be passed to the **DO WHILE** command.

notes: The **LOOP** command can always be avoided by restructuring the logic of the command file. Its purpose is to save time by avoiding interpreting commands in large **DO WHILE** constructs.

MODIFY COMMAND [<command file>]

Creates or modifies a command file.

where: **<command file>** is the name of the command file. If it is omitted, the user is prompted for it. In addition to the normal full-screen control operations (CTRL-key), the following functions are also supported.

CTRL-N	inserts a blank line at the cursor position
CTRL-T	deletes a line at the cursor position
CTRL-C	scrolls up
CTRL-R	scrolls down
CTRL-W	exits and writes the changes to disk
CTRL-Q	exits without saving the command file

notes: The creation and modification of large command files is more conveniently done with an editor or word processor.

NOTE <comment>
* <comment>

Used to insert comments into a command file.

> *notes:*   The comment is not echoed to the output
> device. (See the **REMARK** command.)

READ

Enters full-screen mode for editing of all fields associated
with outstanding **GET**s of previously issued **@** commands.

> *notes:*   Variables associated with the **GET** phrase of
> the **@** command to be edited with the **READ**
> must be field names of the database in use, or
> character memory variables.
>
>   **SET SCREEN ON** must be in effect to
> allow the editing of variables associated with
> the **@** commands.
>
>   If **SET FORMAT TO SCREEN** is in
> effect, then the **READ** may be issued to edit
> the variables associated with outstanding
> **GET**s.
>
>   If **SET FORMAT TO PRINT** is in effect,
> then the **READ** is ignored.
>
>   If **SET FORMAT TO <format file>** is in
> effect, then all **@** commands in the associated
> format file are executed prior to entering the
> full-screen edit mode. In a sense this is
> equivalent to
>
> > **DO <format file>**
> > **READ**

examples:

```
SET ESCAPE ON
SET FORMAT TO MAINMENU
READ
SET FORMAT TO SCREEN
ACCEPT "Enter Menu Selection" TO MENU
DO WHILE .NOT. FILE(!(MENU+'.FMT'))
    @ 23,1 SAY 'Invalid Selection' GET MENU
    READ
ENDDO
SET FORMAT TO &MENU
READ
SET FORMAT TO SCREEN
ACCEPT "Enter Operation" TO OPERATION
DO WHILE .NOT. FILE(!(&OPERATION+'.CMD'))
```

@ 23,1 SAY 'Invalid Operation' GET OPERATION
READ
ENDDO
DO &OPERATION

> This segment of a command file might be used to drive a "menu driven" application. The screen is formatted with the "main menu" by the first **READ**. The user is then prompted to enter the name of a "submenu" which is presumably explained in the main menu. If the specified menu is not in the directory, the user is allowed to edit his choice with the next **READ** command. The screen is then formatted by the next **READ** command with the specified menu. The user is then prompted to enter the names of a command file, presumably explained in the menu just displayed, and prompted until a valid command file is indicated. The command file is then executed.

RELEASE <memory variable list>
RELEASE ALL

> Releases (i.e., deletes) a set of memory variables.
> *where*:   **<memory variable list>** denotes a set of memory variables be released.
>
>   **ALL** indicates that all memory variables are to be released.
> *example*:   **RELEASE TIME,DATE,STATUS**
>
> Releases three memory variables.

REMARK <comment>

> Echoes a comment to to the output device. (See the **NOTE** command.)

RESTORE FROM <file>

> This restores a previously saved set of memory variables.
> *where*:   **<file>** is the name of a memory variable file containing a set of previously **SAVE**d memory variables.

notes: Used in conjunction with the **SAVE** command, this is a means of passing parameters between command files.

    If the command files make extensive use of memory variables, they may be **SAVE**d and **RESTORE**d by the invoked command file.

SAVE <file>

Saves the current set of memory variables.

where: **<file>** denotes the name of the memory variable file in which to save the current memory variables.

notes: Used in conjunction with the **RESTORE** command, this is a means of passing parameters between command files.

    If the command files makes extensive use of memory variables, then they may be **SAVE**d and **RESTORE**d by the invoked command file.

STORE <expression> TO <memory variable>

Evaluates the expression and places the value in the designated memory variable.

where: **<expression>** is a logical, numeric, or character expression.

    <memory variable> denotes the name of the receiving memory variable.

notes: The memory variable may be subsequently referred to from command files by name or a macro substitution (&).

    This is the quick way to pass parameters between command files.

examples: **STORE 'SMITH'$!(NAME) TO NAMEOK**

Stores **T** in the logical memory variable **NAMEOK** if the character string **SMITH** is a substring of the **NAME** field. Note that the **NAME** field was translated to uppercase.

STORE BALANCE+DEPOSIT TO NEWBALANCE

Stores the sum of the **BALANCE** and **DE-POSIT** field in the numeric memory variable **NEWBALANCE**

STORE TRIM(LAST:NAME) TO CURR:NAME

Stores the **LAST:NAME** field in the character memory variable **CURR:NAME** with trailing blanks removed.

WAIT [TO <memory variable>]

Pauses until a single keystroke is entered from the keyboard.

where: **TO <memory variable>** specifies a memory variable to receive the character.

notes: If a control character is entered, the memory variable will be set to a blank.

examples: **ACCEPT 'enter name and press any key to continue' TO NAME**

WAIT

Accepts a name and waits for a keystroke from the terminal.

@ 23,1 SAY 'do you wish to continue (Y/N)'
WAIT TO ANSWER
IF !(ANSWER)='N'
      CANCEL
ENDIF

Cancels the command file if the user entered **n** or **N** to the prompt.

Common dBASE II Error Messages

BAD NAME FIELD

The field name supplied does not conform to conventions.

BAD TYPE FIELD

The field type must be **C** for character, **N** for numeric, or **L** for logical type.

BAD DECIMAL WIDTH FIELD or BAD WIDTH FIELD

The width of the field being defined is invalid.

COMMAND FILE CANNOT BE FOUND

The command file does not exist or was misspelled.

DATA ITEM NOT FOUND

The command contains an undefined database field name.

DISK IS FULL

The disk cannot hold any more data.

"FIELD" PHRASE NOT FOUND

See PHRASE ERRORS below.

FILE DOES NOT EXIST

The file name given is not on the disk or is misspelled.

FILE IS CURRENTLY OPEN

Operation requires that the file be closed via USE or CLEAR.

ILLEGAL VARIABLE NAME

The variable name supplied does not conform to conventions.

INDEX FILE CANNOT BE OPENED

Index file name was probably misspelled or does not exist.

MACRO IS NOT A CHARACTER STRING

Macros must be character-type memory variables.

NO "FOR" PHRASE

See PHRASE ERRORS below.

NO "FROM" PHRASE

See PHRASE ERRORS below.

NO FIND

The specified key was not found.

"ON" PHRASE NOT FOUND

See PHRASE ERRORS below.

RECORD NOT IN INDEX

The database was probably updated when the index was not in use. The index will have to be recreated.

RECORD OUT OF RANGE

The record number provided does not exist in the database.

SOURCE AND DESTINATION DATA TYPES ARE DIFFERENT

Attempt to REPLACE a field of one data type with another type of data.

*** SYNTAX ERROR ***

The command given does not conform to the definition.

"TO" PHRASE NOT FOUND

See PHRASE ERRORS below.

"WITH" PHRASE NOT FOUND

See PHRASE ERRORS below.

*** UNKNOWN COMMAND

The command issued is not a dBASE II command.

PHRASE ERRORS

Some commands require certain "phrases" in order to work correctly. If a phrase is missing, an error message is issued stating what type of phrase was expected for the command. The same message may be issued if correct phrases are provided but do not follow the order according to the command definition.

Correcting Erroneous Statements

dBASE II provides an error correction facility for commands that are incorrect. After the type of error is listed, the correction dialogue might look like the following:

CORRECT AND RETRY (Y/N)? — **Y** allows statement correction.

CHANGE FROM : — A character string with the error is typed.

CHANGE TO : — The correct character string is typed.

MORE CORRECTIONS (Y/N)? — **Y** allows more corrections to the statement.